GW01157625

Analogue Guide

Los Angeles

Contents

Los Angeles

—Welcome to Analogue Los Angeles

Los Angeles is somewhat of an elusive place. Sceptics are quick to dismiss it as a barren desert of freeways and strip malls, populated by a people whose civic duty ends at their driveway. This is probably not entirely untrue. Yet this glittery sprawl has captured the imagination of sufficient fortune, fame and sun-seekers to turn it into America's second city.

Founded as 'El Pueblo de la Reyna de los Angeles' in 1781 by the Spanish governor of California, LA was still a small town when the railway arrived in 1876. By the 1920s the city had turned into a bustling metropolis of over a million people, boasting film studios and thriving banks. The advent of the car and the conspiratorial demise of its streetcars, famously portrayed in *Who Framed Roger Rabbit*, turned LA into the archetype mid-century suburban American dreamscape.

Decades of immigration and reinvention have created America's most diverse suburban landscape, interspersed with pockets of distinct metropolitan flair: Abbot Kinney Boulevard in the midst of Venice's bohemian patchwork of wooden cottages, sophisticated West 3rd Street in the Fairfax District and übercool Sunset Junction in Silver Lake. And then there's Downtown. The former heart of the city is morphing into a strangely urban incarnation of LA life: a diverse neighbourhood with metro stations at busy intersections and loft apartments in former bank buildings.

We've jumped into the driver's seat to unearth the most fascinating bits that this enthralling city has to offer, with photography and maps throughout. Enjoy!

Neighbourhoods

Santa Monica —p8
Suburbia meets the Pacific in this picture perfect seaside town of manicured lawns, upmarket retail and a touch of beach bohemia.

HOLLYWOOD HILLS

HO

BEVERLY HILLS

CENTURY CITY

BRENTWOOD

WESTSIDE

SANTA MONICA

CULVER CITY

VENICE

Venice —p24
In America's Venice—complete with canals—neighbourhood life revolves around upmarket Abbot Kinney Boulevard.

SANTA MONICA BAY

N

3 kilometres

LOS ANGELES INTER

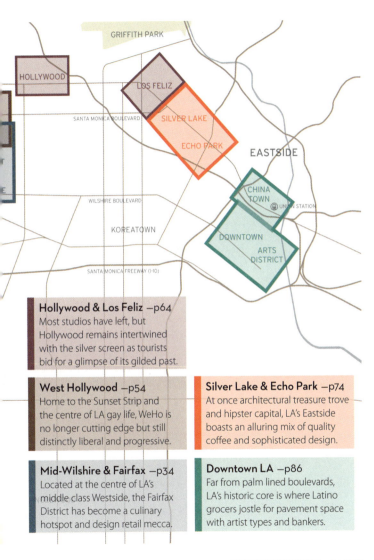

GRIFFITH PARK

HOLLYWOOD

LOS FELIZ

SILVER LAKE

ECHO PARK

SANTA MONICA BOULEVARD

EASTSIDE

CHINA TOWN

UNION STATION

WILSHIRE BOULEVARD

KOREATOWN

DOWNTOWN

ARTS DISTRICT

SANTA MONICA FREEWAY (I-10)

Hollywood & Los Feliz —p64
Most studios have left, but Hollywood remains intertwined with the silver screen as tourists bid for a glimpse of its gilded past.

West Hollywood —p54
Home to the Sunset Strip and the centre of LA gay life, WeHo is no longer cutting edge but still distinctly liberal and progressive.

Mid-Wilshire & Fairfax —p34
Located at the centre of LA's middle class Westside, the Fairfax District has become a culinary hotspot and design retail mecca.

Silver Lake & Echo Park —p74
At once architectural treasure trove and hipster capital, LA's Eastside boasts an alluring mix of quality coffee and sophisticated design.

Downtown LA —p86
Far from palm lined boulevards, LA's historic core is where Latino grocers jostle for pavement space with artist types and bankers.

Santa Monica

—Postcard Pretty Beach Town

Overlooking the shimmering Pacific through palm lined Palisades Park (p15), affluent Santa Monica, a city in its own right, comes close to what many would consider the perfect seaside town. The climate plays its part, and unlike the scorching summer days further inland, seaside breezes keep the temperature agreeable almost all year round. The one catch, perhaps, would be that decades of wealth and perfect weather have made it staunchly resilient to the cutting edge.

Founded in 1875, Santa Monica was envisioned as the maritime gateway to the fledgling city of Los Angeles. Those ambitions were not fulfilled, but Santa Monica instead grew into an early 20th century seaside resort complete with several amusement piers. Santa Monica Pier, the only remaining one, is a touristy affair, but a defining feature of the city's coastline.

Santa Monica's commercial life is centred on Downtown, where today's Third Street Promenade was created in an extensive 1980s effort to revitalise the faltering area. Although a commercial success, its offerings are fairly predictable. Just a few blocks north, Montana Avenue is a distinctly more upscale, yet interesting and walkable stretch of small shops and eateries.

At the northern edge of 4th Street, the Santa Monica Stairs, a popular outdoor workout spot for local *sportifs*, lead into the hilly Pacific Palisades. Main Street and the Ocean Park neighbourhood just south of Downtown still maintain patches of California yoga-esque bohemia, but the area is also increasingly popular with executives and celebrities. To the east, Santa Monica gives way to the manicured lawns of Brentwood's suburbia.

12th St

11th St

10th St

9th St

Carlyle Av

Caffe Luxxe (p16)

Lincoln Blvd

Georgina Av

7th St

7th St

NORTH OF MONTANA

6th St

5th St

SANTA MONICA

4th St

Entrada Dr

Santa Monica Stairs

3rd St

Adelaide Drive

Annenberg Community Beach House

San Vicente Blvd

2nd St

Montana Av

Ocean Av

Idaho Av

Palisades Av

Washington Av

Georgina Av

Alta Av

Palisades Park

Marguerita Av

Ocean Av

Mabery Rd

2

Pacific Coast Highway

(+) EAMES HOUSE.

Reel Inn (Malibu)

5

6

▲

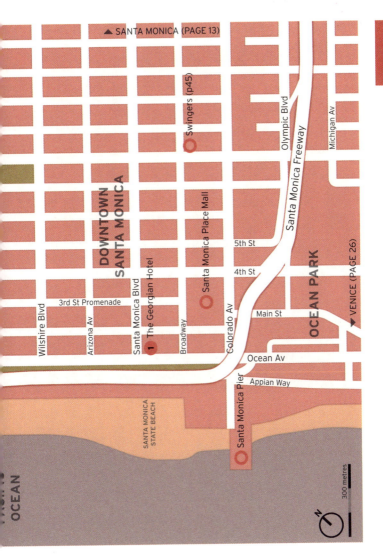

▲ SANTA MONICA (PAGE 13)

Swingers (p45)

DOWNTOWN
SANTA MONICA

Olympic Blvd

Michigan Av

Santa Monica Freeway

Santa Monica Place Mall

5th St

4th St

OCEAN PARK

▼ VENICE (PAGE 26)

Wilshire Blvd

3rd St Promenade

Arizona Av

Santa Monica Blvd

1 The Georgian Hotel

Broadway

Colorado Av

Main St

Ocean Av

Appian Way

Santa Monica Pier

SANTA MONICA
STATE BEACH

OCEAN

300 metres

N

GETTY CENTRE

BRENTWOOD

Franklin St
Stanford St
Yale St
Harvard St
Princeton St
26th St
25th St
24th St
23rd St
22nd St
21th St
20th St
19th St
18th St
17th St
16th St
15th St
14th St
Euclid St

San Vicente Blvd
South Burlingame Av
Moreno Av
Avondale Av
Brentwood Terrace

Caffe Luxxe **3**
Farmshop **7**

NORTH OF MONTANA

Georgina Av
Carlyle Av
Marguerita Av
Alta Av
Montana Av
Aero Theatre **9**
Idaho Av
Washington Av

Gehry House

▼ SANTA MONICA (PAGE 10)

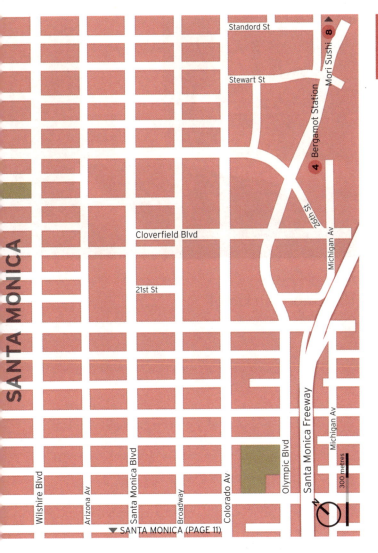

SANTA MONICA

Standord St

Stewart St

Bergamot Station

Mori Sushi

8

4

29th St

Michigan Av

Cloverfield Blvd

21st St

Wilshire Blvd

Arizona Av

Santa Monica Blvd

Broadway

Colorado Av

Olympic Blvd

Santa Monica Freeway

Michigan Av

300 metres

▼ SANTA MONICA (PAGE 11)

Art Deco Seaside Hotel

The Georgian Hotel

1 1415 Ocean Avenue
+1 310 395 9945
georgianhotel.com
Doubles from $310/night incl. tax

The elegant Georgian Hotel first opened its doors in 1933. The hotel's design is a fusion of Romanesque and Art Deco styles and perfectly encapsulates the zeitgeist of LA's early twentieth century coastal expansion. Once the breezy summer preserve of celebrities looking to escape scalding temperatures further inland, the hotel, with its unique ocean views, continues to charm visitors to this day. Rooms are tastefully appointed and Aveda products allow for a pampering shower. A fabulous breakfast is on offer daily on the oceanside patio.

Oceanside Park

Palisades Park

2 Between Ocean Avenue and Pacific Coast Highway

+1 310 458 8644

Public access.

A thin stretch of elegant palm trees and trimmed grass alongside Ocean Avenue, the Palisades Park is a perfect microcosm of Santa Monica life. The park offers ample opportunity for an exhilarating run or gentle stroll overlooking the Pacific, Malibu and the Santa Monica Mountains in the distance. Windward, public stairs descend the sandstone bluffs to Santa Monica's broad sandy beach.

Luxurious Cappuccino

Caffe Luxxe

3 225 26th Street
+1 310 440 7802
caffeluxxe.com
Open daily 7am-6pm.

A fresh and elegant Northern Italian style café in the Brentwood Country Mart, an upmarket retail hub in this otherwise residential part of LA, Caffe Luxxe's artisanally crafted espresso based drinks go hand in hand with the delectable pastries and sandwiches on offer. Tables spill onto the outdoor deck facing 26th Street, where patrons relax with the morning paper and a cappuccino while basking in the sun. The café's second location, on pretty Montana Avenue, is a prime option to be enjoyed after some Santa Monica shopping or sun bathing.

Gallery Cluster

Bergamot Station

 2525 Michigan Avenue
+1 310 453 7535
bergamotstation.com
Closed Sun/Mon. Open Tue-Fri
10am-6pm; Sat 11am-5.30pm. Free
admission.

Bergamot Station was originally a stop on the Red Line trolley connecting Santa Monica to Los Angeles. After the demise of the trolleys in the 1950s, the space underwent stints as a celery packing plant and an ice making facility before morphing into its present incarnation as a multifaceted contemporary art gallery hub.

Public Beachside Pool

Annenberg Community Beach House

 415 Pacific Coast Highway; footbridge across Pacific Coast Highway at Montana Avenue

+1 310 458 4904

beachhouse.smgov.net

Open daily Nov-Mar 8.30am-5.30pm; Apr/Oct 8.30am-6.30pm; May-Sep 8.30am-8.30pm. Pool open May-Sep. Free admission. Pool $10.

A public institution on a prime stretch of beach with dashing views of the Pacific, the Annenberg Community Beach House is a fabulous spot for those seeking breakfast *al fresco*, a spate of yoga or a dip in the oceanside pool. The beach-side café's sunny orange umbrellas feel just as summery in January as in July.

Malibu Seafood

Reel Inn

 18661 Pacific Coast Highway; approx. 4 miles from Santa Monica

+1 310 456 8221

reelinnmalibu.com

Open daily 11am-9pm.

For a casual seaside getaway within relative proximity to LA, head out to Malibu's Reel Inn, a fabulous fish restaurant on the fringes of the Pacific. Order your desired creature of the deep to taste before heading out to the patio with a beer and relaxing in the sway of the soothing ocean breeze.

to LUNCH WITH EAMES?!

Country Mart Cuisine

Farmshop

 225 26th Street
+1 310 566 2400
farmshopla.com
Open daily. Breakfast Mon-Fri
7.30am-11am. Lunch Mon-Fri 11.15am-
2.30pm. Brunch Sat/Sun 8am-2pm.
Dinner Wed-Sun 5.30pm-9.30pm.

Adjacent to its own organic market inside the Brentwood Country Mart, Farmshop takes full advantage of California's staggering array of fresh produce. A fabulous spot for brunch, the space is all clean lines, highlighted by capri blue banquettes. The on-site bakery produces fresh loaves, perfect for warming up the palate alongside a glass of artisanal California Cabernet, before the main course is served.

LA Sushi Highlight

Mori Sushi

 11500 West Pico Boulevard
+1 310 479 3939

morisushi.org

Closed Sun. Lunch Mon-Fri noon-
2.30pm. Dinner Mon-Sat 6pm-10pm.

On a relatively nondescript stretch of Pico Boulevard, Mori prepares some of the freshest, most authentic sushi in LA. The lunch sushi special is divine, and green tea (in powder, not tea bag form) is served in hand made Japanese earthenware cups. The serene blonde plywood and paper lamp dotted interior allows for a calm conducive to fully focusing on the tasty morsels adorning your wooden *geta*.

Mid-Century Movie Classic

Aero Theatre

9 1328 Montana Avenue
+1 310 260 1528
americancinematheque.com
Regular screenings. Tickets $11

When it first opened in 1939, the Aero Theatre operated round the clock, serving the entertainment needs of neighbouring Douglas Aircraft Company's employees. It has since become a neighbourhood treasure and continues to screen art-house films, both classic and contemporary. The theatre's original Art-Deco features were refurbished in 2005.

Venice

—Upmarket Counterculture

Santa Monica's eccentric sibling to the south, Venice is perhaps most famous for its beach life and countercultural legacy—epitomised by the carnevalesque atmosphere of Ocean Front Walk. Only a few blocks inland, the mania gives way to a sea of residential streets and backyard "walk streets" lined with small, though increasingly luxuriously decked out cottages.

Venice, or rather the "Venice of America", was the brainchild of tobacco millionaire Abbot Kinney. After a fallout with his Ocean Park developer partner, Kinney moved south and in 1905 opened an amusement district and pier near the site of today's Muscle Beach. To top things off, Kinney also developed a beach resort town interspersed with several miles of canals. Bridges were modelled after and gondoliers imported from its Italian namesake. After Kinney's death from lung cancer, Venice was annexed by the City of Los Angeles which, true to itself, proceeded to pave over most of the canals. In the 1950s, the neglected neighbourhood became a hotbed of progressive art and design, attracting the likes of Charles and Ray Eames.

Faithful to its liberal tendencies to this day, Venice is now one of LA's wealthiest neighbourhoods. While peddlers and fortunetellers continue to hawk their wares to aging hippies and boardwalk tourists, the highlight of contemporary Venice is undoubtedly Abbot Kinney Boulevard, a mile-long stretch of innovative retail and interesting culinary options. As central Venice has become increasingly pricey, creative minds have directed their attention to the area's Oakwood section, a fairly mixed working class neighbourhood further inland.

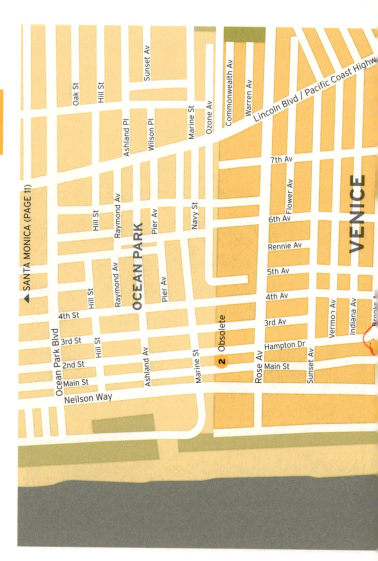

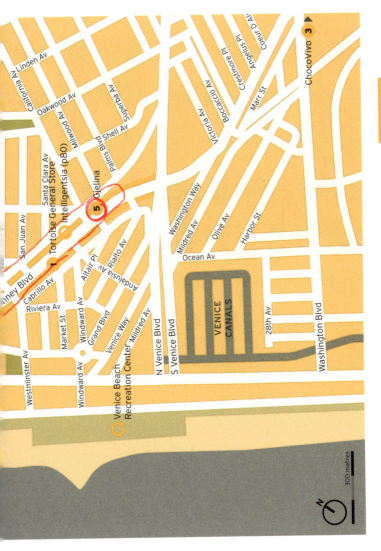

California Av
Linden Av
Oakwood Av
Milwood Av
Santa Clara Av
San Juan Av
Shell Av
Superba Av
Palms Blvd
Gjelina
Intelligentsia (p30)
Tortoise General Store
1
5
Kinney Blvd
Cabrillo Av
Riviera Av
Altair Pl
Andalusia Av
Rialto Av
Market St
Windward Av
Grand Blvd
Venice Way
Westminster Av
Windward Av
Mildred Av
Venice Beach
Recreation Center
N Venice Blvd
S Venice Blvd
Ocean Av
Mildred Av
Washington Way
Olive Av
Victoria Av
Boccaccio Pl
Crestmore Pl
Angelus Pl
Coeur D Al
Marr St
Harbor St
ChocoVivo 3
VENICE
CANALS
28th Av
Washington Blvd

300 metres

N

Japanese Design

Tortoise General Store

1 1208 Abbot Kinney Boulevard
+1 310 314 8448
tortoisegeneralstore.com
Closed Mon. Open Tue-Sat 11.30am-6.30pm; Sun noon-6pm.

A fabulous range of Japanese houseware, kitchenware, stationary and books await the lucky customer at the Tortoise General Store. The bright and inviting shop spills into a charming back garden and workshop, where pottery is created. Whether you're searching for a Matcha Tea Whisk Stand, an iron ornament schnauzer or a crafted baby rattle, it will be available at the Tortoise.

Arts & Design

Obsolete

 222 Main Street
+1 310 399 0024

obsoleteinc.com

Closed Tue/Sun. Open Mon/Wed-Sat
11am-6pm.

At the crossroads between an art and design gallery and a store, Obsolete offers a feast for the eyes on otherwise fairly predictable Main Street. Serendipitous finds and exquisite objets d'art, including the original maquettes of ships from the 1800s, adorn every corner of the shop. If you're looking to unearth a treasure, this is definitely the place to go.

Stone Ground Chocolate

ChocoVivo

3 12469 Washington Boulevard
+1 310 463 7878
chocovivo.com
Open daily 11am-9pm.

A wonderful new addition to the burgeoning Washington Boulevard culinary scene, ChocoVivo specialises in stone ground chocolate produced in the style of the Mayans and Aztecs. Chocolates are all 65-100 percent pure cacao, including some blends the likes of ginger and vanilla, with no additives whatsoever. Choco's owner, Patricia Tsai, can guide you through a chocolate tasting, or you can simply purchase your favourite bar to be enjoyed later with an espresso.

Global Flavours

Axe

 1009 Abbot Kinney Boulevard
+1 310 664 9787

axerestaurant.com

Closed Mon/Tue. Breakfast Wed-Fri
9am-11am. Lunch Wed-Fri 11.30am-
3pm. Brunch Sat/Sun 9.30am-3pm.
Dinner Wed/Thu 6pm-10pm; Fri/Sat
6pm-10.30pm; Sun 6pm-9.30pm.

Named after a Yoruban salutation, Axe is the brainchild of chef and owner Joanna Moore. Designed in a light and modern mix of congona and black acacia woods softened by handmade lamps, Axe is one of Venice's most attractive haunts. Open windows and a lovely back patio allow for a constant whiff of Pacific breeze. Dishes are fresh, delicious and inspired, taking full advantage of the diversity of fruits and vegetables sprouting locally. Wines incorporate robust California and Old World selections.

Abbot Kinney Classic

Gjelina

 1429 Abbot Kinney Boulevard
+1 310 450 1429

gjelina.com

Open daily. Mon-Fri 11.30am-
midnight; Sat/Sun 9am-midnight.

This sophisticated Abbot Kinney institution buzzes with energy round the clock. Dimly lit, modern and slick, Gjelina is a great choice for those searching for casual elegance. Pizza is thin crusted, mouth watering and backed up by a strong wine list. Small and large fusion cuisine plates are equally tempting. The back patio is a great place to people watch while luxuriating in your *kumamoto* oysters and champagne.

Mid-Wilshire & Fairfax

—Museum Row and Culinary Canyon

Compared with its conspicuous neighbours—ritzy Beverly Hills and liberal West Hollywood—the Fairfax District has a fairly democratic feel. Mostly known for its Farmers Market (p42) today, the neighbourhood has long been a focal point of Jewish life on LA's Westside. The Miracle Mile, the stretch of Wilshire Boulevard bounding the Fairfax District to the south, garnered its name from the commercial success of its 1920s department stores.

Covered by dairy farms and bean fields until the early 20th century, the Fairfax District came to life in the 1930s and 40s when predominantly Jewish middle class families settled in the area, establishing the delis and shops of what became known as the "Kosher Canyon" of Fairfax Avenue. The Farmers Market, dating back to 1934, retained a fairly local profile until 2001 when the opening of The Grove, a brashly commercial outdoor mall on an adjacent plot, began to attract a more suburban crowd. The local culinary scene has taken its cues from the continued success of the market. West 3rd Street and Beverly Boulevard in particular are notable for the quality of their eateries and retail offerings.

Further south, Wilshire Boulevard was little more than an unpaved farm road until the 1920s. Foreseeing that it would eventually become a major thoroughfare linking Downtown LA with Santa Monica, developer A.W. Ross saw potential for a new commercial district designed around the automobile. The plan involved such novelties as dedicated left-turns and even prescribed building forms and advertising lettering, contributing to the emerging styles of Art Deco and Streamline Moderne. Today, the area is more notable for its museums, including LACMA (p40).

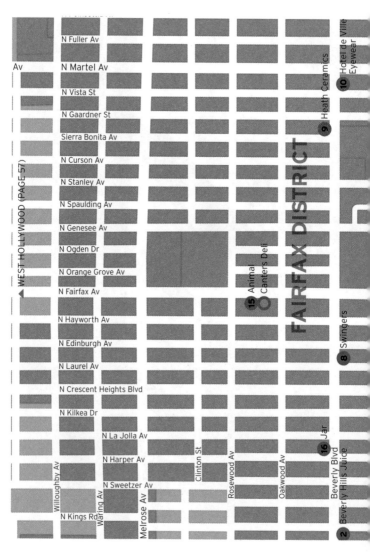

Av

N Fuller Av

N Martel Av

N Vista St

N Gaardner St

Sierra Bonita Av

N Curson Av

N Stanley Av

N Spaulding Av

N Genesee Av

N Ogden Dr

N Orange Grove Av

N Fairfax Av

N Hayworth Av

N Edinburgh Av

N Laurel Av

N Crescent Heights Blvd

N Kilkea Dr

N La Jolla Av

N Harper Av

N Sweetzer Av

N Kings Rd

Willoughby Av

Waring Av

Melrose Av

WEST HOLLYWOOD (PAGE 57)

FAIRFAX DISTRICT

Clinton St

Rosewood Av

Oakwood Av

Beverly Blvd

9 Heath Ceramics

10 Hotel de Ville Eyewear

15 Animal / Canters Deli

8 Swingers

16 Jar

Beverly Hills Juice

2

MID-WILSHIRE & FAIRFAX   PAGE 37

Mid-Century Beverly Hills

Avalon Hotel

1 9400 West Olympic Boulevard
+1 310 277 5221
avalonbeverlyhills.com
Doubles from $357/night incl. tax

A mid-century retro-glam hotel in the thick of Beverly Hills, the Avalon exudes SoCal flair. Set around a gorgeous bubble shaped pool dotted with airy cabanas, the hotel's rooms are outfitted with pieces by Isamu Noguchi and Charles Eames. The in-house restaurant, Oliverio, serves Italian cuisine in a California setting at outdoor tables surrounding the pool.

Raw Juice

Beverly Hills Juice

2 8382 Beverly Boulevard
+1 323 655 8300
beverlyhillsjuice.com
Closed Sun. Open Mon-Fri 7am-6pm;
Sat 9am-6pm.

Opened in 1975 by maverick juicer David Otto, Beverly Hills Juice has buffed up scores of local residents with its naturally powerful set of raw concoctions ever since. Raw and Pressed juices, Banana Manna shakes (a vegan mix of banana and almond, cacao or sunflower) and the mighty duo of wheatgrass and E3Live Brain On, all pack a powerful punch. Topping it off, Beverly Hills Juice sources most of its organic ingredients locally.

MONO p. ⟩ (handwritten)

Art and Eames

LACMA

 5905 Wilshire Boulevard
+1 323 857 6000

lacma.org

Closed Wed. Mon/Tue/Thu 11am–
5pm; Fri 11am-8pm; Sat/Sun 10am-
7pm. Admission ~~$15~~

$20, $16 STUDENTS. (handwritten)
$25 $21. (handwritten)

FREE AFTER 3pm Mon-Fri (handwritten)

The West Coast's largest museum is also one of the world's premier art galleries, housing more than 100,000 works by major artists spanning a vast range of styles and historical periods. LACMA hosts exhibitions at the forefront of the art world year round, as well as talks, live music events, films and opportunities for research. After soaking in some culture, retire to the museum's front patio where you can enjoy a cup of coffee on a colourful Ray Eames chair.

Cutting Edge Gallery

ACE Gallery

4 5514 Wilshire Boulevard
+1 323 935 3388
acegallery.net
Closed Sun. Open Mon-Sat 10am-6pm. Free admission

The ACE Gallery exhibits cutting edge contemporary and modern art accentuated by its visually appealing second floor location in a Magic Mile glam 1930s tower, complete with staffed vintage elevator. Artists the likes of Robert Rauschenberg and Julien Schnabel are regularly exhibited and the gallery makes for a refreshingly intimate setting when compared with its larger Museum Mile neighbours. The ACE Gallery also has a Beverly Hills location (pictured above).

Fairfax Foodie Spot

Farmers Market

 6333 West 3rd Street
+1 323 933 9211
farmersmarketla.com
Open daily. Mon-Fri 9am-9pm; Sat
9am-8pm; Sun 10am-7pm.

A 1934 institution, the Farmers Market originated on a plot of land known as "Gilmore Island" where farmers would sell fruit, vegetables and flowers out of the back of trucks. The site is now occupied by an eclectic and elaborate selection of high quality food stands, cafés and shops. With outdoor seating throughout, you can sample everything from tacos at Loteria Grill to *Gado Gado* at Singapore's Banana Leaf—naturally followed by an espresso quaffed at Single Origin (see next page).

Farmers Market Coffee

Single Origin Coffee

 6333 West 3rd Street, Stall #316
+1 323 761 7976
socoffeela.com
Open daily. Mon-Sat 8am-9pm; Sun 8am-7.30pm.

Undoubtedly one of the highlights of LA's famed Farmers Market (see previous page), Single Origin Coffee serves up a distinguished brew at the *al fresco* stall it shares with the Short Cake bakery. SO is the ideal spot to grab a post-lunch espresso after exploring the market's diverse culinary repertoire. Sit at one of the high stools surrounding the café's exuberantly tiled façade and enjoy your cappuccino and croissant with a section of the LA times.

Café and Gallery Space

Paper or Plastik Café

7   5772 West Pico Boulevard
+1 323 935 0268
paperorplastikcafe.com
Open daily. 7am-10pm.

Paper or Plastik, an avant-garde industrial style café, merges the realms of distinguished espresso and visual and performing arts. From the café you can catch a glimpse of the adjoining dance studio/art space, overseen by design team Anya and Yasha Michelson and their daughter Marina. Paper doubles as a restaurant and collaborates with quality driven roasters and local bakeries as well as small production wineries.

Contemporary Classic Diner

Swingers

8 8020 Beverly Boulevard
+1 323 653 5858
swingersdiner.com
Open daily 6.30am-4am.

A playful mid-century style diner with contemporary zest, Swingers cooks up a brunchy storm well into the wee hours of the morning. The restaurant sources organic produce whenever possible, with several healthy options available. Multi-grain banana pancakes, jerk chicken omelette, tofu *chilaquiles* and soy banana shakes share space with the usual lox and bagel type suspects.

Beauty Meets Functionality

Heath Ceramics

 7525 Beverly Boulevard
+1 323 965 0800
heathceramics.com
Open daily. Mon-Wed/Fri/Sat 10am-6pm; Thu 10am-7pm; Sun noon-6pm.

Founded in 1948 by potter Edith Heath, Heath Ceramics grew to become one of the most iconic names in California design. Heath's wonderfully earthy single kiln fired tableware and tiles, still hand crafted in Sausalito, California, are available for purchase at the attractive LA flagship store. A testament to their lasting quality and artistic value, Heath's designs are on display at LACMA (p40) and MoMA. In addition to phenomenal ceramics, the shop also sells books on craft and design.

Vintage Eyewear Boutique

Hotel de Ville Eyewear

 7422 Beverly Boulevard
+1 323 634 9911
hoteldevilleeyewear.com
Open daily. Mon-Fri 11am-7pm; Sat
10.30am-6pm; Sun 11am-5pm.

Should you fancy a spanking new pair of retro-chic specs, look no further than Hotel de Ville Eyewear. The classic-meets-contemporary shop offers a plethora of interesting frames, including sunglasses—*de rigueur* given that LA experiences close to 365 days of sunshine a year—in a setting dedicated to vintage aspects of LA culture. After purchasing your shades, head over to Jar (p53) where you can show them off over a glass of champagne.

3rd Street Fashion
South Willard

 8038 West 3rd Street
+1 323 653 6153
southwillard.com
Open daily. Mon-Sat noon-6pm; Sun noon-5pm.

Elegant menswear boutique South Willard is a distinctive staple of 3rd Street, one of LA's most eclectically sophisticated retail stretches. In addition to refined but rugged menswear, South Willard also sells a range of handsome accessories, including shoes, ceramics, books and lamps—a must for the cosmopolitan urban male.

That Potent Powder

Matcha Source

🔵 8036 West 3rd Street
+1 310 845 9392

matchasource.com

Closed Sat/Sun. Open Mon-Fri 11am-5pm; or by appointment.

Alissa White's potent matcha boutique takes tea to a new level. While offering a sumptuous selection of the seductive and health enhancing eponymous Japanese green tea powder, Matcha Source also sells a panoply of matcha inspired accoutrements, the likes of splendid fog linen trays, hand crafted in Japan, and feather-light wooden tea whisks. Drop by for a taste and you'll be sure to leave with a package or two.

Treasure Trove

OK

 8303 West 3rd Street
+1 323 653 3501
okstore.la
Open daily. Mon-Sat 11am-6.30pm;
Sun noon-6pm.

A treasure chest of visual delights, OK sells everything from vintage telephones to oversized Milan *gigante* erasers in a playful, understated setting. Dive into the shop's dinnerware section for classics by Heath (p46) or cave into your desire for an electric blue Comme des Garçons wallet. The "moderne chess set" and "space pen" are classics in the making, while the soft leather Dosa pouches are hand crafted in LA.

Nautical Delight

Son of a Gun

 8370 West 3rd Street
+1 323 782 9033
sonofagunrestaurant.com
Open daily. Lunch Mon-Fri 11.30am-
2.30pm. Dinner Sun-Thu 6pm-11pm;
Fri/Sat 6pm-midnight.

From the same duo behind Animal
(p52), comes seafood-centric Son
of a Gun—a more recent addition
to the culinary hotbed that is 3rd
Street. The menu is top notch, while
an unfussy and ebullient nautical
vein prevails. Offerings change
seasonally, with such delights as
alligator schnitzel, king crab leg
and amberjack crudo making a
showing. To whet your appetite,
grassy bar oysters on the half shell
and a *coupe* of champagne are *de
rigueur*.

Shaking up the Kitchen

Animal

15 435 North Fairfax Avenue
+1 323 782 9225
animalrestaurant.com
Open daily. Sun-Thu 6pm-11pm; Fri/
Sat 6pm-midnight.

In 2008, Chefs Jon Shook and Vinny Dotolo, the self-proclaimed "dudes with a pan", shook up the LA dining scene with the opening of this animal-centric bastion of culinary might in the midst of the Fairfax District's "Kosher Canyon". The daily changing menu is influenced by local, seasonal and organic ingredients. The restaurant's relaxed atmosphere and soft lines offer a pleasing counterbalance to the serious aplomb of the dishes.

West Coast Flair

Jar

 8225 Beverly Boulevard
+1 323 655 6566

thejar.com

Open daily. Dinner Mon-Sun from 5.30pm. Brunch Sun from 10am.

A bastion of nouvelle American cuisine, Jar's décor is as pleasing as the fruits of its kitchen. Soft lighting, wood panelling and 50s style simple elegance set the stage for a relaxing meal or an intimate tête-a-tête at the bar. Chef Suzanne Tracht's repertoire includes the Kansas City Steak and Oysters on the half shell with black pepper ponzu. West Coast flair and flavour at its best.

West Hollywood

—Progressive Central LA

Nestled on the southern edge of the Hollywood Hills, half way between Beverly Hills and Hollywood, West Hollywood is reputed for its liberal disposition and the Sunset Strip's legacy as a playground for the Hollywood elite.

The sloped expanse that today is West Hollywood was dominated by ranches, notably the Rancho La Brea, until far into 19th century. With the advent the railway, the area found itself at the favourable crossroads between thriving Los Angeles and the Pacific Ocean, leading to the foundation of a railroad worker settlement called Sherman. Its freewheeling reputation and the fact that it remained unincorporated and not part of the City of Los Angeles, made it greatly suitable for trades and pastimes shy of government intrusion. Out of reach of the LAPD, interwar Sunset Boulevard turned into the notorious "Strip" of liquor-friendly nightclubs and gambling establishments. By the 1960s the Sunset Strip had lost its favour with movie stars and in moved music groups, and an increasingly well-heeled clientele of entertainment executives and tourists.

With the Sunset Strip having become distinctly more tame and "Westside" in feel, the interesting bits of West Hollywood are increasingly found in its more residential side streets and less prominent avenues, such as those of the Norma Triangle. Nevertheless, West Hollywood's liberal legacy lives on in its reincarnation as a focal point of gay and lesbian life in Los Angeles. In 1984, its residents elected to incorporate West Hollywood as an independent city to protect and nurture its progressive lifestyle.

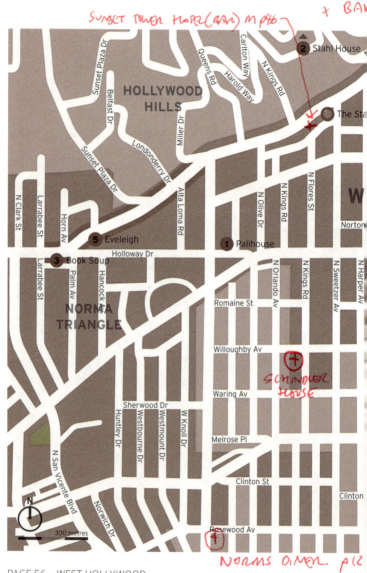

SUNSET TOWER HOTEL (BAR) M P46 — + BA

2 Stahl House

The Sta

Carlton Way

Queens Rd

Harold Way

N Kings Rd

Sunset Plaza Dr

Belfast Dr

HOLLYWOOD HILLS

Londonderry Dr

Miller Dr

Sunset Plaza Dr

Alta Loma Rd

N Clark St

Larrabee St

Horn Av

Larrabee St

Palm Av

Hancock

5 Eveleigh

3 Book Soup

Holloway Dr

N Olive Dr

N Kings Rd

N Flores St

W

Norton

1 Palihouse

N Orlando Av

N Kings Rd

N Sweetzer Av

N Harper Av

Romaine St

NORMA TRIANGLE

Willoughby Av

⊕ SCHINDLER HOUSE

Waring Av

Sherwood Dr

Huntley Dr

Westbourne Dr

Westmount Dr

W Knoll Dr

Melrose Pl

N San Vicente Blvd

Norwich Dr

Clinton St

Clinton

N

300 metres

Rosewood Av

NORMS DINER. P12

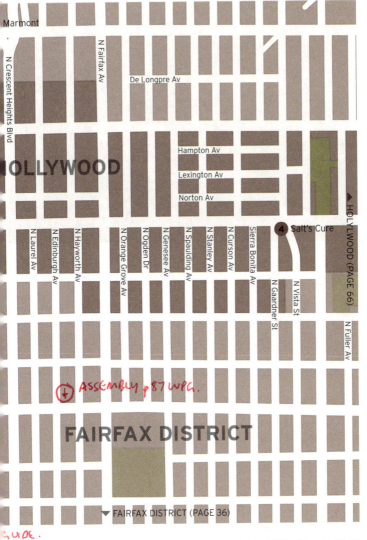

OUSC . #21. KOENIG.

Marmont

N Crescent Heights Blvd

N Fairfax Av

De Longpre Av

HOLLYWOOD

Hampton Av

Lexington Av

Norton Av

N Laurel Av

N Edinburgh Av

N Hayworth Av

N Orange Grove Av

N Ogden Dr

N Genesee Av

N Spaulding Av

N Stanley Av

N Curson Av

Sierra Bonita Av

N Gaardner St

N Vista St

N Fuller Av

4 Salt's Cure

HOLLYWOOD (PAGE 66)

ASSEMBLY p 87 WEG.

FAIRFAX DISTRICT

▼ FAIRFAX DISTRICT (PAGE 36)

GUIDE.

The British Touch

Palihouse

8465 Holloway Drive
+1 323 656 4100
palihouse.com
Doubles from $421/night incl. tax

LA meets the UK at this plush urban hotel and residence. Nestled in fairly walkable Norman Triangle, Palihouse's prime location is seamlessly combined with the comforts of a long-term dwelling, on-site courtyard brasserie and comfy lounge. Suites and residences are meticulously decorated with laid-back panache, and come equipped with kitchens. A tastefully relaxed option for those choosing to make WeHo their LA home for a spell.

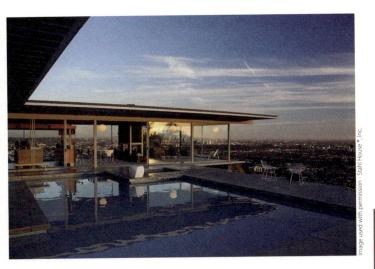

Image used with permission - Stahl House® Inc.

Modern Architecture Classic

Stahl House

2 1635 Woods Drive
+1 323 744 1635

stahlhouse.com

Refer to website for schedule of tours. Admission $60 ($35/person for two or more).

In the aftermath of World War II, Arts & Architecture magazine commissioned America's architectural avant-garde to create a series of efficient yet inexpensive model homes. Many of these Case Study Houses, designed by the likes of Richard Neutra and Eero Saarinen, were built in the Los Angeles area. Overlooking the city from the Hollywood Hills, Pierre Koenig's Stahl House, or Case Study House #22, is perhaps the most iconic representation of Los Angeles modernism. The house is privately owned but open for visits upon arrangement.

Books with a View

Book Soup

 8818 Sunset Boulevard
+1 310 659 3110

booksoup.com

Open daily. Mon-Sat 9am-10pm; Sun 9am-7pm.

Perched on a curve of Sunset Blvd overhanging dramatic views of the sprawl, this LA classic stocks a fabulous selection of fiction, non-fiction, travel, art and design books, as well as a comprehensive newsstand appendix. The shop also stocks a curated selection of books focusing on all things Angelino. A definite must for those craving a Raymond Chandler noir, a book on Googie-style architecture or simply the latest *Paris Match*. If you're feeling peckish after all that browsing, head over to Eveleigh (p62) for brunch.

Porcine Delight

Salt's Cure

 7494 Santa Monica Boulevard
+1 323 850 7258

saltscure.com

Open daily. Lunch/Brunch 9am-3pm.
Dinner 5.30pm-10.30pm.

Salt's Cure, an organic hipster hangout that works as well for brunch as for dinner, specialises in all things porcine. Originally intended as a sustainable butcher shop, the restaurant is now one of the highlights of the WeHo brunch scene. Owners and chefs Christopher Phelps and Zachary Walters ensure that eggs are perfectly fluffed, home fries thick and wholesome, and all produce, down to the sparkling wine, is sourced in California. The space is modern and minimalist, encompassing slick wood panelling and various hues of slate.

Antepodean Angels

Eveleigh

 8752 Sunset Boulevard
+1 424 239 1630

theeveleigh.com

Open daily. Brunch Sat/Sun 10am-3pm. Dinner Sun-Wed 5pm-10pm; Thu-Sat 5pm-11pm. Late Night Menu: Sun-Wed 10pm-11pm; Thu-Sat 11pm-12:30am.

A scintillating brunch-to-dinner spot on the Sunset Strip, Australian owned Eveleigh brings a slice of the Antipodes to the city of angels. The restaurant spills onto a back terrace allowing for classic Sunset Boulevard views of the city's expanse. At night, enjoy a cheese board and a glass of champers overlooking the sparkling carpet of lights beneath.

Glamorous Dinner and Drinks

Bar Marmont

6 8221 West Sunset Boulevard
+1 323 656 1010
chateaumarmont.com
Open daily 6pm-2am.

Hedged at the mouth of the winding road leading to the chateau-like hotel from which it derives its name, Bar Marmont is a playful cocktail den/restaurant at the heart of the Sunset Strip. Swing by for a Martini amid the Hollywood types or for a casual dinner in an ambience redolent with the neighbourhood's lustre. For a Hollywood A-list power drinking session head up to the bar at the Chateau.

Hollywood & Los Feliz

—Home to the Movies

Stretched over the lower flanks of the Hollywood Hills, Hollywood is closely associated with American cinema and the glamorous lives of the movie stars. This being despite the fact that hardly a major film has been shot in the area for decades.

Hollywood sprung up in the late 19th century, in what were then barley fields and citrus groves. By 1915, the area was the movie capital of America, and, since the 1950s, also home to a thriving music industry. The 1956 Capitol Records Building is a glamorous reminder of this legacy. At the same time, however, film studios began to radiate out to more spacious terrain across the hills. The Walk of Fame, created in 1958, introduced Hollywood's long uphill struggle to live up to its glamorous reputation. Though not entirely devoid of movie related industries, tourists bidding for a glimpse of its gilded past are the area's mainstay today. Though one might be tempted to steal a glance at Hollywood Boulevard, most of the neighbourhood's finds are tucked away in its side streets.

Los Feliz, just adjacent to the east, was once part of the extensive Rancho Los Feliz, an 18th century land grant by the then Spanish governor. Subsequent owners donated the hilly north of the area, now Griffith Park (p68), to the public and turned what remained into the elegant suburb of Los Feliz. Just a stone's throw from Hollywood, the area had its share of movie making; it was home to Disney's original animation studio, but gained prominence as an upmarket residential neighbourhood for executive-type residents. Frank Lloyd Wright's Ennis House, just off Hollywood Boulevard, is a spectacular reminder of this legacy.

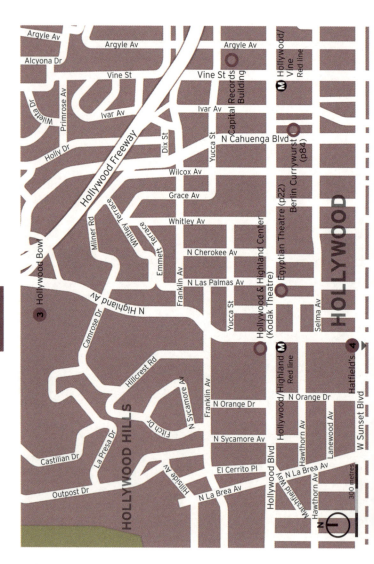

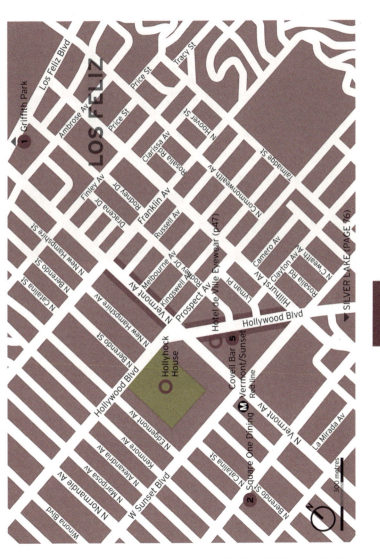

Urban Wilderness

Griffith Park

1 North of Los Feliz and Hollywood
+1 323 913 4688
Open daily 5am-10.30pm.

One of the largest urban parks in America, Griffith Park is a stunningly rugged expanse of shrubland extending from the northern edges of Los Feliz. The terrain was donated to the public by industrialist Colonel Griffith in the late 19th century. The park is interspersed with more manicured bits and leisure attractions, including the famous Griffith Observatory and the Greek Theatre, an outdoor amphitheatre. Both are quite touristy, but the park's extensive path network makes for great hiking and spectacular views over the city.

Los Feliz Brunch

Square One Dining

2 4854 Fountain Avenue
+1 323 661 1109
squareonedining.com
Ⓜ Vermont/Sunset ●
Open daily 8.30am-3pm.

An excellent brunch spot, Square One Dining serves up fluffy pancakes, scrumptious eggs and delicious sandwiches daily for breakfast and lunch. The indoor area is cosy and convivial, while the outdoor back deck has a relaxed feel. The restaurant mainly sources local and organic produce with consistently delicious results.

Stunning Performing Arts Venue

Hollywood Bowl

 2301 North Highland Avenue
+1 323 850 2058

hollywoodbowl.com

Regular performances. Refer to
website for program.

A summer evening concert at the Hollywood Bowl is a quintessential LA experience. Dramatically nestled in the Hollywood Hills with prime views of the Hollywood sign, the Bowl hosts world renowned classical and contemporary musicians, in addition to the LA Philharmonic's summer season. Bring a picnic and a bottle of wine along or simply book a table at one of the Bowl's *al fresco* restaurants.

Elegant Modern Dining

Hatfield's

8370 West 3rd Street
+1 323 782 9033
hatfieldsrestaurant.com
Open daily. Dinner Sun-Thu 6pm-
10pm; Fri 6pm-10:30pm; Sat 5:30pm-
10:30pm; Sun 5:30pm-9:30pm.

Hatfield's serves innovative new-American cuisine in a sophisticated and refreshing setting. The locally sourced menu is strongly influenced by seasonal dynamics and dishes burst with succulent flavour. The décor, complete with honeycomb inspired lighting, is soothing and refined. Hatfield's is an absolute must for foodies, as well as for those in search of a high calibre dining experience.

Neighbourhood Bar

Covell Bar

 4628 Hollywood Boulevard
+1 323 660 4400

barcovell.com

Ⓜ Vermont/Sunset 🔴

Open daily. Sun-Thu 5pm-midnight;
Fri/Sat 5pm-2am.

Covell Bar is a laid back Los Feliz wine bar offering some outstanding oenology. Owner Dustin Lancaster made the move from Silver Lake institution Café Stella (p85) in 2010, bringing the best of the wine world to Los Feliz. Wine program director Matthew Kaner ensures that staff are intimately versed on all wines on offer. The atmosphere is mellow but sophisticated and French inspired small plates, designed to pair with the wines, are also available.

Silver Lake & Echo Park

—Modernist Architecture and Hipsters

Owing more to their grungy appearance than blue-collar pedigree, Silver Lake and Echo Park often find themselves casually mixed in with LA's "Eastside", despite being located to the west of the LA River. Nonetheless, these neighbourhoods off West Sunset Boulevard, with their eclectic mix of hipsters and creative types, are as Eastside as can be.

The hilly area north of Downtown LA was largely pastoral until the late 19th century, when the rapidly growing city expanded north along West Sunset Boulevard. In 1909, Echo Park, then called Edendale, was home to LA's first silent film studio. After the movie industry had moved west to Hollywood only a few years later, both areas developed the progressive qualities that they enjoy to this day—Echo Park is said to have attracted many political radicals, while the leafy hills of Silver Lake became a testing ground for some of the leading figures of architectural modernism.

Today, Silver Lake is one of *the* hipster capitals, boasting of course all the amenities that come with it. Mix this with the neighbourhood's architectural and design heritage and the result is an alluring blend of top-notch coffee outlets and sophisticated furniture and design stores. Most of these are clustered around the Sunset Junction crossroads and along West Sunset Boulevard, the neighbourhood's fairly dense and walkable main thoroughfare. Beyond lies an attractive, hilly incarnation of LA suburbia—interspersed with prime examples of modernist architecture.

SILVER LAKE

LOS FELIZ (PAGE 67)

Landa St

Windsor Av

Redcliff St

Cumberland Av

Manzanita St

Fernwood Av

Hyperion Av

Griffith Park Blvd

Maltman Av

1 Lodging 323

Bates Av

Talmadge St

Fountain Av

N Hoover St

N Talmadge St

W Sunset Blvd

4 Mohawk General Store

SUNSET JUNCTION

Manzanita St

2 Cafe Stella

1 Intelligentsia

7 Berlin Currywurst

6 Forage

8 **5** **3**

The Cheese Store
of Silver Lake

Hyperion Av

Golden Gate Av

Michaltorena St

N Commonwealth Av

N Hoover St

Sanborn Av

Lucile Av

Edgecliffe Dr

Maltman Av

La Mirada Av

Lyman Pl

N Virgil Av

N Westmoreland Av

Santa Monica Blvd

Willow Brook Av

N Madison Av

N Lockwood Av

Burns Av

Normal Av

Monroe St

Lucile Av

Maltman Av

Ⓜ Vermont/Santa Monica
Red line

NEUTRA VDL RESEARCH HOUSE

Eastside Apartments

Lodging 323

1 1801 1/2 Edgecliffe Drive
+1 323 661 5440
houseinsilverlake.com
Ⓜ Vermont/Santa Monica ●
One bedroom apartment from
$200/night incl. tax Three nights
minimum stay.

Lodging 323 offers a range of comfortable apartment-style dwellings, providing an excellent alternative to a hotel for those preferring to feel instantly at home in their new urban setting. The apartments, located near the summit of one Silver Lake's hills, are light, modern, tastefully decorated and come with fully equipped kitchens.

Rococo Brew

Lamill

2 1636 Silver Lake Boulevard
+1 323 663 4441
lamillcoffee.com
Open daily. Sun-Thu 7am-10pm; Fri/
Sat 7am-11pm.

A striking red exterior and huge glass doors lead to a modern lounge-type café with rococo touches, where you can pair Lamill's signature coffee with a slice of cake or enjoy a light meal with a glass of cava, followed by a luxurious double shot affogato. Outdoor seating, on a leafy corner of one of the neighbourhood's more residential pockets, is an additional draw.

Chicago Coffee Import

Intelligentsia

3 3922 West Sunset Boulevard
+1 323 663 6173
intelligentsiacoffee.com
Ⓜ Vermont/Santa Monica ●
Open daily. Sun-Wed 6am-8pm; Thu-Sat 6am-11pm.

One of LA's premier coffee spots, Chicago based hipster haven Intelligentsia offers cutting edge brew in the artisanally tiled Sunset Junction outdoor complex, which also houses Café Stella (p85) and The Cheese Store of Silver lake (p82). Undoubtedly a place to see and to be seen, Intelligentsia's tiled bar is an excellent spot to catch up on the latest news while losing yourself in the depths of a perfectly formed flat white.

Sunset Boulevard Find

Mohawk General Store

4 4011 West Sunset Boulevard
+1 323 669 1601
mohawkgeneralstore.net
Ⓜ Vermont/Santa Monica ●
Open daily. Mon-Sat 11am-7pm; Sun
11am-6pm.

An eclectic mix of expertly curated design, home accessory and fashion gems awaits the visitor to the Mohawk General Store. From African salad bowls to arts and crafts style pottery and the latest in urban fashion by favourites the likes of FOUND and A.P.C., the range of must have objects is alluring. A soothing décor and knowledgeable staff heighten the experience.

Epicurean Silver Lake

The Cheese Store of Silver Lake

5 3926 West Sunset Boulevard
+1 323 644 7511
cheesestoresl.com
Ⓜ Vermont/Santa Monica ⬤
Open daily. Mon-Sat 10am-6pm; Sun 11am-5pm.

An epicurean highlight, The Cheese Store of Silver Lake offers a storehouse of gastronomical treats sourced from near and far. The dizzying array of goat, sheep, cow and blue cheeses is complemented by an excellent selection of wines spanning the globe. Owner Chris Pollen hand selects all the items on offer, ensuring a uniformly high calibre foodie experience.

Organic Cuisine Rapide

Forage

6 3823 West Sunset Boulevard
+1 323 663 6885
foragela.com
Ⓜ Vermont/Santa Monica ●
Closed Sun/Mon. Lunch Tue-Fri
11.30am-3pm; Sat 11am-4pm. Dinner
Tue-Sat 5.30pm-9.30pm.

Jason Kim merges haute cuisine with *cuisine rapide* at this Silver Lake eatery. A popular lunch and dinner spot, Forage sources its organic ingredients from local farmer's markets, whipping up a tantalising storm of freshly prepared modern California dishes in a casual setting. Service is cafeteria style and the décor is minimalist chic.

A True Berliner

Berlin Currywurst

7 3827 West Sunset Boulevard
+1 323 663 1989
berlincurrywurst.com
Ⓜ Vermont/Santa Monica ●
Open daily. Mon-Thu noon-10pm; Fri/
Sat noon-11pm; Sun noon-8pm.

Founded by true Berliners, Berlin Currywurst brings the city's celebrated urban street food to Silver Lake's palm tree dotted avenues. Concocted in a variety of styles, choose from a range of all-natural *wurst* including *Geflügelbratwurst* and tofu *Kielbasa*, pepped up by a variety of sauces, all spiced to taste. Sausages are served with fresh German farmer's bread and can be enjoyed in the contemporary Berlin-style shop or on its distinctly Californian front patio.

Douce France
Café Stella

8 3932 West Sunset Boulevard
+1 323 666 0265
cafestella.com
M Vermont/Santa Monica ●
Open daily. Mon 6pm-11pm; Tue-Sat
9am-3pm, 6pm-11pm; Sun 9am-3pm,
6pm-10pm. Bar open daily 6pm-late.

A fabulous brasserie in Sunset Junction, one of Silver Lake's most interesting corners, Café Stella serves up French classics round the clock in a modern Gallic setting. *Tartare de thon*, *coq au vin* and *steak frites* pair beautifully with an excellent selection of wine and beer. And nothing can beat the effervescent king of all aperitifs, the *kir royal*, taken beneath the SoCal palms.

Downtown LA

—LA's Old and New Urban Centre

Think of Los Angeles, and what comes to mind are the palm lined boulevards and manicured lawns of the Westside. Downtown LA could not be more different. Though still far from its apogee, the area has come a long way from being associated with crime-ridden and desolate 1970s Skid Row. Today, Downtown is where artist types linger in cafés and bankers jostle for pavement space with Latino grocers and jewellery traders.

The city of LA has its roots at the northern fringes of what is now Downtown—today the site of picturesque yet rather touristy Olvera Street. By 1930, Downtown had turned into the core of a booming metropolis, boasting grand hotels, glamorous movie palaces and opulent banks. However, increasing car ownership following World War II led to the area's rapid decline, as LA became its suburban self. Everything changed in 1999, when developers were encouraged to transform the area's stunning architecture into residential lofts.

The former banks of the Historic Core now house art galleries and cafés, and an increasing array of culinary options. Broadway also boasts the largest concentration of vintage movie theatres in the country. Now mostly defunct, many had survived past decades as Spanish language venues. To the west, Victorian Bunker Hill was razed in the 1950s to make way for today's financial district and the arts and performance venues of Grand Avenue.

To the east, the industrial and railroad buildings of the Arts (formerly Warehouse) District, an artistic enclave since the 1970s, have since become popular with professionals. Chinatown and Little Tokyo, both primarily cultural and shopping areas, are nods to California's long tradition of immigration from the Far East.

MORPHOSIS BUILD

W Temple St

▲ CHINATOWN (PAGE 90)

City Hall

Ⓜ Civic Center/Grand Park
Red/Purple lines

Little Tokyo/Arts Dist
Gold

+ THE BROAD
PL. WP.

W 1st St

Walt Disney
Concert Hall

12

E 1st St

S Grand Av

S Olive St

S Hill St

S Broadway St

S Spring St

S Main St

E Los Angeles St

6 Little

The
BROAD

10 FILM

MOCA

Downtown
Independent

S San Pedro St

S Flower St

S Hope St

W 3rd St

GRAND
CENTRAL
MARKET
Macey

E 3rd St

Wall St

W 4th St

E 4th St

2 Yoga Circle Downtown

Winston St

DOWNTOWN

W 5th St

E 5th St

Ⓜ Pershing Square
Red/Purple lines

PERSHING
SQUARE

3 Spring for Coffee

San Julian St

1 The Standard

W 6th St

E 6th St

9 Mignon

Wilshire Blvd

**FASHION
DISTRICT**

Ⓜ 7th Street/
Metro Center
Red/Purple/Blue/Expo lines

W 7th St

11 Bottega Louie

E 7th St

PHSP

W 8th St

VERVE
COFFEE

E 8th St

Eastern Columbia
Building

Spring for Coffee (p93)

Santee St

FICINE

W 9th St

13

E 9th St

N

Pattern Bar

E 10th St

300 metres

W 10th St

ACE
HOTEL.

BLACK TOP
COFFEE
MP39

ANGELES
RIVER

+ WURST.

7 Wurstküche
Traction Av

4 Handsome
Coffee Roasters
P94

ARTS DISTRICT

ROW!

8 Church & State

+ BESTIA
ITALIAN

E 7th St

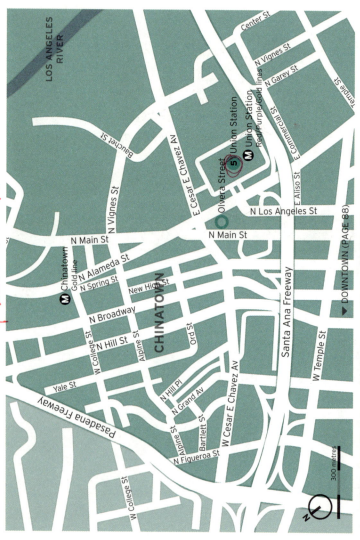

1960s Galore

The Standard Downtown

550 South Flower Street
+1 213 892 8080
standardhotels.com
Ⓜ 7th Street/Metro Center ●●●●
Doubles from $254/night incl. tax

Set in a glamorous James Bond-style 1960s tower block, The Standard offers all the retro-chic trappings that have come to be associated with an André Balazs venture. Jaw dropping views of the Downtown LA skyline complement the mid-century décor. Enjoy a nightcap at the roof bar before retiring to your room.

Grand Yoga Space

Yoga Circle Downtown

 400 South Main Street #S05
+1 213 620 1040

yogacircledowntown.com

Ⓜ Pershing Square ● ●

Classes daily. Classes from $16. Mat rental $1.

An independent yoga studio set in a cavernous old bank building, Yoga Circle Downtown allows you to catch up on your *asanas* while absorbing some of LA's turn of the century charm. Owner Knekoh Frugé, at the vanguard of the Downtown LA scene, is a fantastic instructor and creates a welcoming environment.

Neighborhood Café

Spring for Coffee

3 548 South Spring Street
+1 213 268 5775
springforcoffee.com

Ⓜ Pershing Square ● ●
Open daily. Mon-Fri 6.30am-8pm;
Sat 7am-8pm; Sun 7.30am-5pm.

Feisty little café and Downtown coffee pioneer Spring for Coffee specializes in excellent hand-crafted espresso drinks in the thick of the Old Bank District. The café has a strong local following, contributing to its playful, artistically charged vibe. Grab a cappuccino and take a stroll around the neighbourhood while absorbing its architectural marvels.

Well Groomed Roasters

Handsome Coffee Roasters

(4) 582 Mateo Street
+1 323 606 3593
handsomecoffee.com
Ⓜ Little Tokyo/Arts District ●
Open daily. Mon-Fri 7am-6pm; Sat/
Sun 8am-6pm.

Nestled in the core of the Arts District, Handsome Roasters offers a stunning set of espresso-based drinks concocted with uncompromising craftsmanship and understated style. Handsome's location on a sun drenched industrial-chic corner, warm minimalist interior design and on-site roasting facility provide the ultimate backdrop for a tête-a-tête with the enthralling bean.

Transcontinental Rail

Union Station

5 800 North Alameda Street
+1 213 683 6875

Ⓜ Union Station ●●●
Open 24 hours.

Opened in 1939, Union Station was one of the last great railway stations built in the US. Its architecture is influenced by both Mission Revival and Streamline Moderne styles, ingeniously melding LA's Spanish past with its, then, modern future. The atmospheric interior, complete with plush leather armchairs in the waiting area, hankers back to the time of intercontinental rail travel. Still LA's main station, Union Station is today primarily serviced by commuter trains and the city's fledgling Metro.

Ramen or Udon?

Little Tokyo

6 West 1st Street, between South Los Angeles Street and South Alameda Street

visitlittletokyo.com

Ⓜ Little Tokyo/Arts District 🟡

Public access.

A National Historic Landmark District and one of the US's three official Japan Towns (all in California), Little Tokyo was once the cultural heart of LA's large Japanese community. The neighbourhood experienced a population decrease after the 1924 Exclusion Act, but was revived in the 1970s when Japan Inc. established several US headquarters in the city. While most Japanese-Americans live elsewhere today, Little Tokyo remains a vibrant community chock full of ramen shops, hotels, Japanese bookshops, supermarkets and bakeries, as well as the Japanese American National Museum.

Arts District Sausage and Beer

Wurstküche

(7) 800 East 3rd Street
+1 213 687 4444
wurstkuche.com
Ⓜ Little Tokyo/Arts District ●
Open daily 11am-midnight. Bar open
until 2am.

A lively beer hall and *Wurst* emporium in the centre of the up-and-coming Arts District, Wurstküche allows patrons to ravish a range of sausages, running the gamut from the classic *Bratwurst* and *Bockwurst*, to more exotic numbers the likes of Vegetarian Mexican Chipotle or Rattlesnake and Rabbit with Jalapeño peppers. To add to the *Lust*, why not wash it all down with a Teutonic draft *Spaten Optimator* quaffed amidst the creeping plants of the outdoor garden.

Arts District Dining

Church & State

8 1850 Industrial Street
+1 213 405 1434
churchandstatebistro.com
Ⓜ Little Tokyo/Arts District ⬤
Open daily. Lunch Mon-Fri 11.30am-
2.30pm. Dinner Mon-Thu 6pm-10pm;
Fri 6pm-11pm; Sat 5.30pm-11pm; Sun
5.30pm-9pm.

Decked out in an industrial space by the railway tracks fringing Downtown's Arts District, Church & State is a contemporary French restaurant catering to the area's burgeoning creative scene. The extensive menu includes classics ranging from *Bouillabaise* to the requisite *Tarte Tatin*. A fabulous selection of French wines covers many of the premier appellations of the *hexagone*.

Wine and Cheese Bar

Mignon

9 128 East 6th Street
+1 213 489 0131
mignonla.com
M Pershing Square 🟣🟠
Open daily 6pm-midnight.

A winning wine and cheese bar, Mignon serves a range of oenological treats by the glass or bottle, including many under-the-radar finds from Europe's lesser-known appellations. Tantalising small plates of Spanish and French origin are also on offer. If you're dropping by for dessert, why not give a glass of *Tokaj Aszu* a whirl, along with the Baked Persimmon, vanilla ice cream and *crème de cassis*.

* SEE A FILM!

Independent Film

Downtown Independent

10 251 South Main Street
+1 213 617 1033
downtownindependent.com
Ⓜ Pershing Square ●●
Screenings daily. Tickets $12

If you fancy an independent flick in a quirky setting while in Downtown, the Independent should fit the bill. The cinema is housed in a retro-1970s Pacific Modernist building, complete with a rooftop deck where ice cold beer can be imbibed while admiring stunning views of Downtown LA.

Opulent LA

Bottega Louie

11 700 South Grand Avenue
+1 213 802 1470
bottegalouie.com

M 7th Street/Metro Center ●●●○
Open daily. Mon-Fri 8am-11:30pm;
Sat 9am-midnight; Sun 9am-11pm.

A wonderfully over-the-top restaurant/café and patisserie, Bottega Louie is a Tinseltown take on an Italian Rococo palace. The establishment's eclectic culinary selection includes everything from roasted organic king salmon and a range of pizzas to *canelés* and red velvet muffins for teatime. Situated at the intersection of the Financial and Old Bank districts, Bottega Louie celebrates Downtown's renaissance with theatrical aplomb.

Gehry Philharmonic

Walt Disney
Concert Hall

 151 South Grand Avenue
+1 323 850 2000

laphil.com

Ⓜ Civic Center ●●

Regular performances. Refer to
website for program.

LA trained Frank Gehry's celebrated
2003 structure scintillates in the
glory of its stainless steel curves and
swooping spaces. The main concert
hall was designed to resemble a
ship's hull and the acoustics by
Yasuhisa Toyota are first rate. The
hall is home to the Los Angeles
Philharmonic and the Los Angeles
Master Chorale.

Urban Bar

Pattern Bar

 100 West 9th Street
+1 213 627 7774

patternbar.com

Ⓜ 7th Street/Metro Center ●●●●

Closed Sun. Mon-Thu noon-midnight;
Fri/Sat noon-2pm.

An ode to fashionable drinking in one of Downtown's ex-bank buildings, Pattern Bar's owners Eduardo Castillo and Alejandro Meza meld the catwalk with Cuban flair. Vintage sewing machines adorn the industrial space's walls, while dim lighting and oversized streetscape views add to the urban vibe. A Latin American inspired menu, complete with *arepas* and tapas mixes perfectly with the excellent fashion-denominated cocktails and selection of wines and beers.

Essentials

Airport Transfer

Most commercial flights arrive at Los Angeles International Airport (LAX), which is located just south of Venice on Santa Monica Bay. There are two main alternatives for moving on from here: rental car or taxi. Most major car rental companies provide shuttle buses just outside Arrivals, taking drivers to dedicated facilities a mile or so away. For those relying on other people's driving skills, taxis are the most realistic alternative, and usually are readily available outside Arrivals. Fares to the nearby Westside are typically $30 or more, and to Hollywood around $50. There is a flat fare of $46.50 in both directions between the airport and Downtown LA (west of Alameda Street). There are also flat fares to the airport from within the city limits of West Hollywood ($40) and Santa Monica ($30-35 north/south of I-10 freeway respectively).

Taxis

Los Angeles is famously spread out, and as such, taxis are not routinely used as a means for going to work or doing one's errands. There are taxi stands at major points of interest, but it is virtually impossible to flag a cab on one of LA's major thoroughfares—outside Downtown and Hollywood, cabbies risk a ticket by picking up passengers in no-parking zones. On the other hand, calling a taxi at short notice is common and relatively hassle free.

Once in the back seat, LA cabs are an efficient means of navigating the sprawl. Fares are roughly in line with those of other major cities (more than New York, less than London), but the numbers can add up very quickly when covering long distances. A ride from Downtown to Santa Monica or Venice will cost about $60 and take 30 minutes, if traffic permits. Drivers are required to accept credit cards for rides over $7.

Nine taxi companies operate throughout LA. The largest one, Yellow Cab (+1 877 733 3305, layellowcab.com) offers convenient back seat credit card screens. A good alternative is Checker Cab (+1 800 300 5007, ineedtaxi.com). For a full list refer to taxicabsla.org.

Car Rental

For those looking to test the tarmac hands on, the easiest and cheapest way is to book a rental car prior to arrival. Significant discounts are often available on online advance bookings for weekly or longer periods. Shorter rentals can be arranged at outlets throughout the city. Most rental companies will be happy to arrange a pick up of the driver in spe.

The speed limit is 25mph in built up areas and 70mph on freeways, unless otherwise posted. It is legal to overtake on the right on multi-lane roads, and to turn "right on red" at traffic lights.

Public Transport

Despite being a city where traffic conditions make for better small talk than the weather, Los Angeles does have a modern and reliable Metro. The catch is that the network is far from extensive. Most usefully, the Red Line links Downtown with touristy Hollywood, stopping within reasonable distance of the more interesting bits of the Eastside (see map p76) along the way. Trains run every 10 minutes between 5am and midnight.

The red "Metro Rapid" buses can be a good alternative for getting around on weekdays when services are fairly frequent. Numbers 704 and 720 run express between Santa Monica and Downtown via Santa Monica and Wilshire Boulevards respectively.

Trains and buses share the same fare structure. A single ticket costs $1.50 but does not include changes, for which a new ticket has to be purchased. Heavy users are encouraged to obtain a "TAP" card which can be loaded with daily ($5), weekly ($20) and monthly ($75) passes, as well as prepaid balances. Refer to p110 for a map of the LA Metro.

Tipping

Tips are an important source of income for most service staff. In restaurants, tip no less than 15%, and 20% or more to reward good service.

Safety

LA's Westside has historically been, and still is, much wealthier and safer than its Eastside and southern suburbs. Also bear in mind that Downtown's Skid Row was a no-go area until just a few years ago.

Index

LOS ANGELES METRO

	Under construction	Scheduled completion
Metro		
		2019
Lightrail		
		2020
		2015/2020
		2019

WEST HOLLYWOOD

BEVERLY HILLS

Fairfax Ave

Wilshire Blvd

Santa Monica Blvd

SANTA MONICA

Wilshire/Fairfax

Westwood/Rancho Park

Palms

La Cienaga/Jefferson

Expo/La Brea

Culver City

Expo/Sepulveda

Expo/Bundy

CULVER CITY

La Cienaga Blvd

La Brea Ave

26th St/Bergamot

17th St/SMC

Venice Blvd

Downtown Santa Monica

VENICE

Hindry

Florence/La Brea

Aviation/Century

Hawthorne/Lennox

LAX

Aviation/LAX

Mariposa

El Segundo

GLENDALE

Southwest Museum

Heritage Sq

LOS FELIZ

wood/
ine

Hollywood/
Western

Vermont/Sunset

Lincoln/Cypress

WOOD

SILVER LAKE

Vermont/Santa Monica

Chinatown

EAST LA

Vermont/Beverly

ECHO PARK

Wilshire/
Vermont

Civic Center/
Grand Park

2nd Pl/
Hope

Union Station

Wilshire/
Western

Wilshire/
Normandie

Westlake/
MacArthur Park

Little Tokyo/Arts District

7th St/Metro Center

Pershing
Square

2nd St/
Broadway

Pico/Aliso

Expo/
Western

23rd St

Pico

Grand

DOWNTOWN LA

ARTS
DISTRICT

Jefferson/USC

San Pedro St

w/MLK

Expo/
Vermont

Expo Park/
USC

Washington

Park

Vernon

w/Slauson

Slauson Ave

Slauson

Florence

Firestone

103rd St/Watts Towers

Vermont/
Athens

Avalon

Western Ave

Normandie Ave

Vermont Ave

Harbor Freeway

Willowbrook

Long Beach

© 2013 Analogue Media

METRO MAP   PAGE 111

Credits

Published by Analogue Media, LLC
244 5th Avenue, Suite 2446, New York, NY 10001, United States

Edited by Alana Stone
Layout & Production by Stefan Horn

For more information about the Analogue Guides series, or to find out about availability and purchase information, please visit analogueguides.com

First Edition 2013
ISBN: 978-0-9838585-2-2

Text, book design and layout copyright © 2013 Analogue Media

All rights reserved. No part of this publication may be reproduced, stored in a retrieval system, or transmitted in any form or by any means electronic, mechanical, photocopying, recording, or otherwise, without prior permission of the publisher and the respective copyright holders.

Every effort has been made to ensure the accuracy of the information in this publication. However, some details are subject to change. The publisher cannot accept responsibility for any loss, injury, inconvenience, or other consequences arising from the use of this book.

Typefaces: Neutraface 2, Myriad Pro and Interstate
Paper: Munken Lynx

Printed in Barcelona by Agpograf, S.A.

- THE BROAD.
  CLOSED MON. OTHER DAYS VARY. 10/11 - 5/8pm

Analogue Media would like to thank all contributing venues, designers, manufacturers, agencies and photographers for their kind permission to reproduce their work in this book.

Cover design by Dustin Wallace
Proofread by John Leisure

Photography credits: all images credited to the listed venues unless stated otherwise. (9) Stefan Horn (17) Spencer Lowell (18) Peter Figen (19/20/21) Spencer Lowell (22) Roger Leatherwood Flickr user rogerbrown22 (25) Stefan Horn (30) Spencer Lowell (31) Saam Gabbay (32) Spencer Lowell (35) Stefan Horn (39) Spencer Lowell (40) Author: Alex Vertikoff / Photo © 2010 Museum Associates/LACMA (42) Spencer Lowell (43) Dana Maione (44) Marina Michelson (45) Spencer Lowell (46) Corey Miller (47/48/50/52) Spencer Lowell (53) Lisa Thompson Photography (55) Stefan Horn (59) Image used with permission - Stahl House ®, Inc. (60/61/62) Spencer Lowell (63) Nikolas Koenig (65) Juan Camilo Bernal / Shutterstock.com (69) Spencer Lowell (70) Courtesy of Los Angeles Philharmonic Association (71) Todd Porter and Diane Cu (72) Spencer Lowell (75) Stefan Horn (80/81/82/84/85) Spencer Lowell (87) Stefan Horn (93) Spencer Lowell (94) Neph & Becky Trejo, eighty eighty-four (95) Michael Lynch (96) Julia Lu (98/99) Spencer Lowell (101) Adam Tyler Brumley (102) Federico Zignani (103) Spencer Lowell.

CLOSED NY 2AM

GETTY CENTRE. CLOSED MON. TUE-FRI + SUN 10.-5.30
SAT 10-9 FREE

NEUTRA VDL RESEARCH HOUSE. SILVER LAKE

2300 SILVER LAKE BLVD. CLOSED! BUM!
See map p.

LACMA GALLERY. RENZO.

SEOUL INTERNATIONAL. NEUTRA, #21. PS4 WAG

SINGLETON HOUSE, MULHOLLAND DR. VIDAL SASSOON

About the Series

—A Modern Take on Simple Elegance

Analogue Guides is a series of curated city guidebooks featuring high quality, unique, low key venues—distilled through the lens of the neighbourhood.

Each neighbourhood is complemented by a concise set of sophisticated listings, including restaurants, cafés, bars, hotels and serendipitous finds, all illustrated with photographs. The listings are supplemented by custom designed, user-friendly maps to facilitate navigation of the cityscape. Venues featured in the guides score high on a number of factors, including locally sourced food, tasteful design, a sophisticated and relaxed atmosphere and independent ownership.

Analogue Guides are designed to complement the internet during pre-travel preparation and smartphones for on-the-ground research. Premium photography and a select choice of venues provide an ideal starting point for pre-travel inspiration. At your destination, the guides serve as portable manuals with detailed neighbourhood maps and clear directions.

The result: a compact, efficient, effervescent manual celebrating the ingenuity of the contemporary metropolis.

- PALM SPRINGS. SELF GUIDED ARCH. TOUR:
  KAUFMAN HOUSE,

- EAMES HOUSE $10 SELF-TOUR. BOOKING REQ.
  CLOSED WED + SUN.   10am - 4pm.
- SCHINDLER HOUSE. 833 N. KINGS RD. W. HOLLYW
  11-6pm. $10. CLOSED MON + TUE   SEE P. 56
              NO RESERVATION REQ.

SANTA MONICA:

ABBOT KINNEY BLVD.
4 + 5. p. 31 + 32 FOR FOOD.

SILVER LAKE

SUNSET JUNCTION CROSSROADS
WEST SUNSET BLVD.

DOWNTOWN

- COFFEE. ③ SPRING FOR COFFEE. p 93
           ④ HANDSOME COFFEE R. p 94
- FILM. ⑥ DOWNTOWN INDEPENDANT. p. 100
- DISNEY CONCERT HALL. ⑫ · p/ 02
- PATTERN BAR. p 105. ⑬.